AROUND THE
WORLD
WITH DARWIN

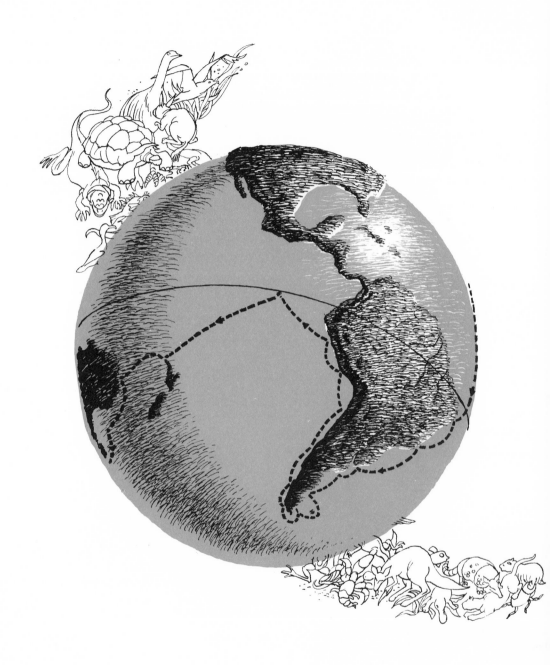

AROUND THE
WORLD
WITH DARWIN

by MILLICENT E. SELSAM

Pictures by Anthony Ravielli

HARPER & BROTHERS
PUBLISHERS, NEW YORK

The British naval ship *Beagle* sailed out of Plymouth Harbor on December 27, 1831. It was going on a trip around the world to make coastal charts for the British navy. The captain was Robert Fitzroy. On board there were sailors, marines, gunners, carpenters, and the usual officers.

There was also a young man on board named Charles Darwin. Captain Fitzroy had invited him to come along on the voyage to study the animals and plants of the different countries they were planning to visit.

Darwin was not specially trained for this work. Most of his college courses had had nothing to do with science. But Charles Darwin had always loved to take long nature walks and collect rocks and insects. While he did not know very much, he had learned to observe things carefully. He was always asking *why* about everything he saw. The earth and all that lived on it were exciting to him. And he had an open mind.

The voyage of the *Beagle* became famous because of the slow patient work of Charles Darwin. What he saw on the voyage led him to a new theory about how so many different animals and plants came to be on the earth. If we follow him as he explores tropical jungles, rides the pampas of Argentina, and crosses the snow-covered Andes, we will see with his eyes what he saw. We will come to understand how he came to think as he did, and why his theory shook the world.

During the two months it took to sail to South America, Darwin was seasick a great deal of the time. He lay in his hammock, miserable, while the ship rolled from side to side.

But whenever the sea was calm, Darwin was busy dragging a net behind the stern of the ship. He spent hours examining the curious sea creatures he found in it.

In Bahia, Brazil, Darwin walked in a tropical forest for the first time. It was hard for him to keep his mind on any one thing. He would start to watch a gorgeous blue butterfly float by, when his eye would be caught by some strange monkey, or some gaudy-looking bird. But after a while, he calmed down, noticed everything, and wrote down what he saw.

The whole country was like a great, wild, over-flowing greenhouse, so different from the neat English countryside he was used to. There were huge trees, vines that climbed up hundreds of feet to the top of the forest. There were beautiful flowers, elegant tree ferns, and enormous ant nests that looked like volcanoes of mud. The forests were full of strange animals, new birds and insects. Darwin felt he was walking through scenes from the *Arabian Nights*.

From Bahia, the *Beagle* sailed south. The next two years were spent surveying the east coast of South America below Rio de Janeiro. While soundings were being taken, Darwin went on shore in Brazil, Uruguay, and Argentina. He roamed the countryside, breaking rocks with his geological hammer, and looking for plants and animals to add to his collection.

He was happy as long as he found a new rock, or a new living thing to examine and describe. Whenever possible, he hired all the boys in a town to collect for him. They kept bringing him strange creatures he had never seen before. And they told him stories of nature wonders he would miss if he didn't go to this or that place. Darwin was often fooled. But he made it a rule to see for himself. A long hard gallop on horseback was nothing to him if at the end of the journey he found something new for his collection.

In Uruguay and Argentina, Darwin met the *gauchos*—the tall, handsome, dashing South American cowboys. They wore bright-colored clothes, great clanking spurs, and knives stuck as daggers at their waists. He admired their wild daring and their skill in hunting. He watched them twirl their lassos around their heads and throw them through the air with sure aim while riding horseback at full speed. When they hunted rheas (South American ostriches), they used *bolas* (two or three round stones covered with leather and connected by a leather thong). They whirled these balls around and then sent them revolving through the air. In an instant, a rhea would roll over and over, its legs lashed together by the thong.

Darwin went riding over the treeless plains or *pampas* of Argentina with the gauchos. He loved their free and independent life in the open air with the sky for a roof and the ground for a table. At any moment, they could pull up their horses and say, "Here we will pass the night." All they needed was water, meat, firewood, and pasture for their horses.

Darwin lived as they did. He spent all day on horseback, ate nothing but meat, drank his maté (tea), smoked his cigar, and went to sleep on the bare ground in the open air.

Darwin found strange new animals on the pampas of Argentina.

Herds of *guanacos* (wild llamas) swarmed over its plains. They were hard to approach, for at the slightest danger the whole herd shrilled notes of alarm, and bolted along some narrow beaten path. Their chief enemy was the *puma,* the lion of South America.

The rabbits of the pampas, *agoutis,* were plentiful.
Darwin often saw them hopping quickly one after the
other across the plains. Their meat was delicious, and
Darwin hunted them for food for the ship's company.

There was also a strange animal called a *viscacha*. It resembles a large rabbit but has bigger gnawing teeth and a long tail. Darwin noticed its habit of collecting everything it found—bones, stones, seeds—and heaping them around the openings of its burrows. When people lost things they searched the heaps in front of the viscacha burrows. They were practically the "Lost and Found Department" of the Argentine pampas.

The *armadillos* were perhaps the strangest of all.
They looked like little armored tanks covered all over
with bony plates. Some of them could roll themselves
up into balls to protect themselves from the attacks
of other animals.

In the red clay earth and rock of the Argentine pampas, Darwin found the remains of animals that were even stranger than the living ones.

He dug up the fossil bones of giant land animals —huge ground sloths, giant armadillos, great beasts that seemed related to the guanacos, and others that were as large as elephants but with teeth like rats.

He imagined South America as it must have looked when these great monsters swarmed over its plains and mountains.

None of these animals was alive any more. They were different from the animals he saw all around him. Yet the fossils resembled the living animals in strange ways.

Darwin wondered about this. Could animals have changed from one kind (species) into another? Could some have died out and others have taken their place? Could the present South American animals be living relatives of these strange monsters whose fossil bones he found?

He sent all the fossil bones home. He didn't expect anybody there to believe a word he said without plenty of proof!

The *Beagle* went to the tip of South America to the land known as Tierra del Fuego or "land of fire." When the ship anchored, the crew saw the fires that had given this place its name. The natives always lit these signal fires when they sighted ships.

Tierra del Fuego was a land of mountains, glaciers, deep inlets, and wild gloomy forests. It was swept by gales, and drenched with rain, sleet, and hail.

Captain Fitzroy sent a party including Darwin on shore to talk to the Fuegians. Darwin was face to face with the first genuine savages he had ever seen! Long black hair streamed around their faces. Their naked bodies and their faces were smeared with black, white, and red paint. Their only clothing was a cape of guanaco skin thrown over the shoulders. They repeated everything the Englishmen said, even though

they didn't understand a word. When one of the Englishmen started to sing a song, the Fuegians almost fell down with surprise.

Darwin saw the wigwams the Fuegians lived in. They were made of a few broken branches stuck in the ground and thatched on one side with tufts of grass and rushes. He watched their women scrape shellfish off the rocks and learned that this was their chief food. At night they slept on the cold bare ground curled up like animals.

Darwin asked himself, "Where did these people come from? Why did a tribe of men leave the fine regions of the north to travel down to this forbidding country?" He decided that in spite of everything, they must be suited to the terrible climate and the poor food or they wouldn't have kept alive for long.

Finally the *Beagle* sailed through the Strait of Magellan to the Pacific side of South America. Here it spent two more years surveying the west coast.

Darwin observed everything—plants, animals, and the habits and customs of the people he met. But he had a very special adventure in Chile.

He was lying on the shore one day when he suddenly felt the ground rock. He was experiencing his first earthquake. It shook his mind as well as his body. The earth that seemed so solid was moving beneath him like a thin crust over jelly.

He went to the nearby town of Concepción. Not a house was left standing. The land around the town was raised two to three feet above sea level. Darwin was seeing what happened when the earth's crust moved. But he was also getting a clue to the past history of the earth. He realized that earthquakes were one of those forces that had been changing the surface of the earth for ages past.

From Valparaiso, Chile, Darwin started out on a trip across the Andes mountains. He traveled with a guide and a mule driver who took care of the ten mules that carried the food, camping equipment, and all the specimens Darwin collected on the way.

The mountain air was clear as crystal. Red and purple rocks were piled in wild masses. Above them was perpetual snow, and below, the rivers shone like silver.

As he climbed the mountains, Darwin studied the rocks. Bit by bit, he built up the story of how this mountain chain was formed. The geologists of his day thought that the Andes had suddenly been thrown up by one great earthquake. But all around him, Darwin saw signs that the huge mountain range had been slowly and gradually raised.

At 7,000 feet, he found some snow-white columns projecting from a cliff. They turned out to be trees of stone. Darwin figured out the story. These trees once grew on the shores of the Atlantic Ocean when long ago it washed the foot of the Andes. (It was now 700 miles away.) Then the shore began to sink and the trees sank with it into the ocean depths. Under the water, minerals filtered in to replace the wood of the trees and gradually turned them to stone. Then the bed of the ocean was lifted again, so that it now stood 7,000 feet above sea level. Darwin had just seen for himself how a tremendous earthquake had raised the land only a few feet! What endless numbers of earthquakes over a long period of time must have taken place to raise the mountains to this level!

At 14,000 feet above sea level, he found shells of animals that had once crawled in the sea.

The high valleys of the Andes were bordered by beds of mud, sand, and stone many thousands of feet thick. Darwin realized that all this mud and sand and stone had been deposited there by mountain rivers. He listened to the noise of the stones rattling over one another in the rushing waters of the rivers. He thought of the endless amount of time that must have passed while the stones rattled down night and day and piled up in the thick beds along the edges of these valleys.

It was becoming clear to him that countless ages of time must have passed while the crust of the earth shifted and moved.

At last the *Beagle* left South America in August, 1835. Darwin was lonely and homesick for the England he had left nearly four years before. Still he looked forward to visiting the islands of the Pacific. The *Beagle* sailed northwest to the Galápagos—a group of volcanic islands situated on the Equator about 600 miles off the west coast of the continent.

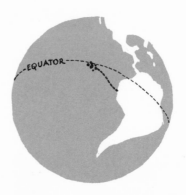

The islands were wild looking and strange. Instead of soil there was black lava—cracked and broken and pitted with small craters. The lava was stone now, but it had once been hot and molten and had boiled out over the rims of the big craters at the tops of the islands. The huge streams of lava had stiffened into the rugged waves of rock Darwin saw before him.

The islands swarmed with strange animals different from any he had seen before! Nowhere else on earth were there such huge tortoises and peculiar lizards. The giant tortoises (*galápagos* in Spanish) gave the islands their name. Some were so large that it took six to eight men to lift them off the ground. When Darwin first saw two of these animals, one was eating a piece of cactus. As he approached, it stared at him and slowly stalked away. The other one gave a deep hiss and drew in its head. These huge reptiles surrounded by the black lava, leafless shrubs, and large cacti seemed like creatures from another planet.

Strange-looking lizards thronged on the rocky ledges overhanging the sea. The black and gray bodies of these miniature dragons called *iguanas* blended perfectly with the lava rock. Darwin opened their stomachs and found that their food was the green seaweed that clung to the rocks at low tide. He was seeing the only sea lizards in the world.

There were big, ugly, yellow-brown land iguanas too, relatives of the sea kind. There were so many of their burrows everywhere that Darwin had trouble finding a spot where he could pitch his tent.

The islands seemed to be dominated by the giant tortoises and the sea and land iguanas.

But the most remarkable thing of all was that the animals and plants on each island of the Galápagos were different!

Darwin learned that the natives of the islands could look at any tortoise and tell from which island it came. When he found this out, he examined the mocking birds he had collected from the different islands. All the birds from one island were of one kind; all from another island were of another kind.

The same was true of the insects he had collected.

His plant collections showed the same thing. On one island, out of 71 plants, 30 were to be found on this island alone. No other island of the group and no other place in the world had such plants.

Darwin knew that the Galápagos Islands were formed by the explosions of undersea volcanoes. If the islands rose in the sea, how did the plants and animals get there? Why should there be such strange new birds, new reptiles, and new plants? Here was a "little world within itself." Yet it wasn't quite that, because in many ways the plants and animals seemed to be related to those of South America. And why were the plants and animals of one island different from those of another?

Darwin puzzled over these questions. If he could answer them, he realized, he would be answering an even bigger question: How had so many different animals and plants come to be on the earth?

From the Galápagos, the *Beagle* sailed halfway across the Pacific to Tahiti. Groves of banana, orange, coconut, and breadfruit trees covered the land sloping to the beach of coral sand. Darwin marveled at these beautiful trees that bore such large nourishing fruit.

But what pleased him most was the people of the islands. He admired their tall, broad-shouldered, athletic bodies and their dark skins. They were so civilized and cultured compared to the poor savages of Tierra del Fuego.

He went on a short excursion to the mountains with two Tahitians. They followed the rocky ledges along a chain of waterfalls in a magnificent mountain gorge. The Tahitians dived into a mountain pool with a small net. Like otters, with their eyes open, they followed the fish into holes and corners and caught them for lunch. When they stopped for dinner, the Tahitians prepared little packages of leaves stuffed with beef, fish, bananas, and other wild fruits and baked them between two layers of hot stones covered with earth. They laid their dinner on a cloth of banana leaves, and with a coconut shell drank the cool

water from the running stream. Then Darwin and his Tahitian friends sat watching the pinnacles of the mountains fade into darkness.

New Zealand was the *Beagle's* next stop. Darwin learned several striking things. The only mammal there was a small rat. A giant flightless bird, the Moa, once dominated New Zealand just as the reptiles still dominated the Galápagos. Here was something else to think about. Another island had queer specimens of life not at all like those on the large continents.

They went on to Australia. There too Darwin wondered about the strange differences between Australian animals and those of the rest of the world. Most of the mammals were *marsupials* like kangaroos. They carried their new-born babies around in the mother's *marsupium* or pouch. Australia had other peculiar mammals too, such as the *duckbill,* or *platypus,* and the *spiny anteater*. Both of these animals laid eggs instead of bearing their young alive like other mammals.

The *Beagle* sailed on to the Keeling Islands in the Indian Ocean. These coral atolls were shaped like doughnuts of land surrounding shallow lagoons.

Darwin examined the living mounds of coral on the side of the islands exposed to the open sea. He marveled that these tiny tender animals could build stony skeletons around themselves from the lime in the sea water, and could grow in the face of the crashing waves.

When Captain Fitzroy made soundings to measure the depth of the water around the coral reefs, he found that there were massive submarine mountains of coral under the atoll. Darwin and he also discovered that living coral grew only in shallow water no deeper than about 180 feet. How then was there dead coral going down for thousands of feet below the living coral?

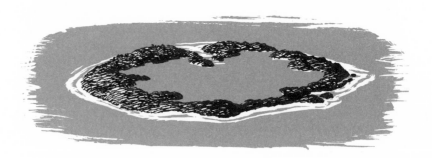

42

Darwin solved this puzzle. The dead coral skeletons now sunk in the depths of the sea must once have lived close to the top of the water. But underneath them the land slowly sank, and as it sank the living coral kept growing upward on the skeletons of the ones below.

Here was another example of the slow gradual changes that had taken place on the earth in past ages.

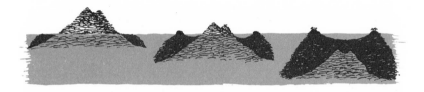

The *Beagle* left the Keeling Islands and continued on its journey by way of the Cape of Good Hope. By now everybody on board was terribly homesick. But they still didn't go directly home. Captain Fitzroy went back to Brazil to complete the entire circle of his voyage around the world as a final check on his measurements.

At long last, the *Beagle* arrived in England, and Darwin stepped ashore almost five years after he had set out!

Charles Darwin spent years after his return working on the tremendous amount of information he had gathered on the voyage. He had collected and sent home tons of plants, rocks, fossils, and skinned and pickled animals. His notebooks were crammed full of observations about the habits of animals, about how they were distributed over the world, about the geology of all the countries he had visited. These notebooks proved to be a real treasure house of facts unknown to most scientists of his day. A group of scientific specialists worked for years on Darwin's collections.

But Darwin was much more than a fact gatherer. Every set of facts raised new questions. The biggest question of all was: Were plants and animals created originally just as they are today, or had they changed from one kind into another?

The things he had seen on the voyage did not fit in with the accepted theories of his time.

Scientists then knew that there were many layers of rock on the earth. They knew there were different kinds of fossils in each layer. But they tried to make this evidence fit their ideas about how the world came to be. The earth, scientists said, looked the way it did because a series of catastrophes such as floods and earthquakes had taken place. After each catastrophe, a whole new set of plants and animals was created. These animals then remained unchanged until the next great catastrophe. That is why, they said, every layer of rocks had a different set of fossils.

There were a few scientists who disagreed. One of them was Charles Lyell. He said that great catastrophes were not necessary to explain the appearance of the earth. Anyone could see for himself, he said, how streams and rivers, earthquakes and volcanoes, wind and rain were shaping the earth from day to day. Given unlimited time—millions of years—these natural forces could gradually have changed the face of the earth.

On the voyage of the *Beagle,* Darwin had seen these things for himself. He came to agree with Lyell that the earth had slowly and gradually changed. It was not thousands—but *millions* of years old.

But Darwin added something more. He said that the living things on the earth have changed too. The huge fossils he had dug up in South America were once animals that had lived there. They had died out. But the new animals that took their place were not "new creations." They were smaller animals, but they were clearly descended from the prehistoric animals.

The problems raised by the Galápagos Islands could only be explained in the same way. By wind and wave, a few of the plants and animals of South America had traveled the 600 miles and arrived at the shores of these islands thousands of years ago. *There they had changed* into the animals and plants he had observed. Even islands of the same group, 50 to 60 miles apart, developed their own peculiar plants and animals.

There was a natural explanation too for the strange animals he had seen in New Zealand and Australia. The animals had come to these islands from nearby islands or continents and then had slowly *changed* into the kinds he had found there.

After years of study, Darwin came to believe that plants and animals had gradually changed or *evolved* from earlier forms of life. They had not been created anew after every catastrophe. Present-day animals were related to the animals of past ages because they came from them.

In 1859, twenty-three years after he returned from the voyage of the *Beagle,* Darwin stated the principle of evolution in a book called *The Origin of Species.* He presented all the evidence he had gathered, and set forth his ideas on how these changes in living things had taken place. This principle has been proved by work done in every branch of biology. Evolution is the cornerstone of the modern science of living things.

Date Due

JUL 23 '65			
AUG 11 '65			
MAY 17 '67			
FE 9 '90			